Hello Kitty

PARTY

First published in the UK by HarperCollins *Children's Books* in 2014

Written by Stella Gurney
with additional material by Gemma Barder
Illustrations by Alys Paterson
All photographic images used under license from Shutterstock.com

1 3 5 7 9 10 8 6 4 2

ISBN: 978-0-00-753109-7

A CIP catalogue record for this title is available from the British Library.
No part of this publication may be reproduced, stored in a retrieval
system or transmitted in any form or by any means, electronic, mechanical,
photocopying, recording or otherwise, without the prior permission of
HarperCollins Publishers Ltd, 77-85 Fulham Palace Road,
Hammersmith, London, W6 8JB.

www.harpercollins.co.uk

Printed and bound in China

Hello Kitty

PARTY

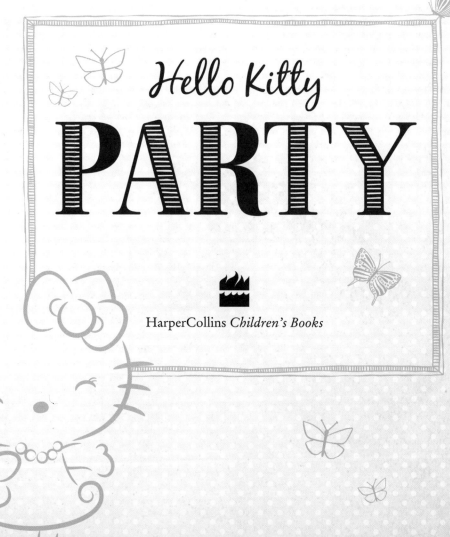

HarperCollins *Children's Books*

CONTENTS

IT'S PARTY TIME!

Hello Kitty loves getting together with friends – there's nothing more fun than a party! So whether you want to hold a vintage tea party or a craft group; create a home spa or set up a book club, my gorgeous guide is crammed with super-cute ideas, fantastic tips and delicious recipes to give your gathering sparkle.

LET'S GET PLANNING!

For younger Hello Kitty fans: lots of the activites, recipes and crafts in this book use sharp or hot equipment like scissors and saucepans. Use your common sense – always ask an adult to help if you are not used to using these things by yourself, or whenever you see this sign.

PREPARE TO BE... PREPARED!

Whatever theme you decide to go for, the key to a successful party is in the planning. It's all too easy to overlook the details, and then flap about in a last-minute panic. Think it through, then make lists, lists and more lists!

FOOD, GLORIOUS FOOD

Food is the heart and soul of any event, so it's worth giving it some thought. You could theme your food to the occasion – for the vintage tea party you might want to serve sandwiches, scones, and lavender shortbread with your tea. For a home spa party why not serve healthy juices and fruit, but provide some banana bread for a treat? For the sass and style party you might want to provide food that won't make a mess on your wonderful new outfits. For book and film parties, you could give your refreshments names that match the novel or movie; maybe a pun on a character's name or the theme of the film? Think about your party, what your guests will like and also what you fancy – it's all about having fun! All the fab recipes in my book can be made in advance, so there's lots of time to take off your pinny and clean up before your guests arrive! Turn to p.92 to get started.

SHOPPING LIST

A good party isn't dependent on spending lots of money, but there are bound to be some things you'll need. Read your recipes through carefully to see if there's anything you need to buy – check to make sure you don't already have them first. Don't actually go shopping until a week or so before the party; by that time you're almost certain to be able to borrow most things that you need.

PLAN AHEAD

Run carefully over all the different elements of your party – it may help to do this with a friend; two heads are better than one. What will you need? Be prepared – make a list! If everyone is planning to do the same craft, make sure you have enough equipment for them all to do it at the same time, or think through whether it will work if they share or use something in turn. Check you have enough chairs, plates, glasses and cutlery, and think about where you will serve your food, and also where it will be eaten. Do you have the right cooking utensils for your recipes? Phew! There's always more to think about than you realise! Hunt around your home for all the items before you beg, borrow, or finally, buy anything that you need.

SWEET SOUNDS

No party is complete without a good soundtrack. Music can set the mood, provide a talking point and cover up any awkward silences, so it's really worth giving some thought to what to play at your event. If you have an MP3 player, you can preset a playlist to last all evening – ask your guests to tell you their favourite song on their RSVP.

BY INVITATION ONLY...

Your guests are the most important ingredient of all. A party for one just isn't fun! Plan carefully who you want to invite – you might want to think about the following as you make your list.

PEOPLE POWER

- Consider how much space you have – too many people can make it feel noisy and crowded; too few, and the room may feel empty and quiet.
- Will the people you want to invite enjoy the party theme? If not, you may want to think about switching the theme – or the guests!
- If the thought of any of the guests at your party makes you feel anxious, cross them off! You want to enjoy yourself, without worrying or feeling judged.
- It's fine to invite people who don't know each other. Remember a stranger is just a friend-in-waiting!

PRECIOUS PAPER

In this age of texts and emails, a real invitation is something to treasure –

especially if it is a beautiful object in its own right. It can brighten up a shelf or mantelpiece and even be framed and hung on the wall as a reminder of a special event. Turn to the next page for some stunning ideas for unique party invites.

GIVING NOTICE

••••••••••••••••••••••••••••••••

Send your invitations out at least a month before the date, so that all your friends have time to plan and keep the date free.

CHECKLIST

••••••••••••••••••••••••••••••••

Once you have written your guest list and sent out your invitations, keep track of who has replied and whether they are coming. Check whether there's anything your guests can't eat, too. That way you can choose recipes everyone will enjoy.

HELLO KITTY'S

VINTAGE TEA PARTY

Date: 9th March

Time: 1pm

Location: Hello Kitty's House

Dress code: Pretty dresses and white gloves!

RSVP: Hello Kitty, by 28th February

HELLO KITTY'S INVITES TO DELIGHT

There's nothing more fun than making something beautiful. These stunning home-made invitation ideas are surprisingly simple but will look seriously impressive when your friends receive them.

You will need:

- pretty paper or fabric
- white or coloured card
- scissors
- glue
- pens and paints

Hello Kitty's
TOP TIP

Don't forget to add all the information about your party: what, when and where!

PERFECT PATTERNS

First, cut your cards to the size you want (fold them in half if you want them to stand up). Next, find some pretty paper or fabric to cut out and add as a border – don't worry about being too neat; rough edges can look stylish! Or why not trace over the templates on the opposite page and then transfer them to your card in your favourite colour combinations?

FLUTTER-BY-HEARTS

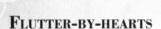

You could also make fab cut-outs to add to your card. What about a fancy flight of butterflies or hearts? Copy or trace one of the templates opposite, then cut out your shapes and stick one half down on to your invitation card, leaving the other unstuck and free to flutter – so cute!

FOLD

FOLD

THE PARTIES

THE VINTAGE TEA PARTY

Ah, the golden age of the tea party – when any self-respecting hostess had embroidered white tablecloths and at least one doily* to her name. Life is such a hustle and bustle these days that those lovely finishing touches usually get overlooked, but Hello Kitty suggests recreating them in all their glory by holding your very own vintage tea party!

*Doily
[dóylee] a decorative lacy mat that is put on plates under cakes or party food to display the food attractively

HOME DECORATING

*First things first – chances are that you'll be holding
your vintage tea party in a modern room. No problem! If
you have some old-fashioned furniture and ornaments,
wonderful, but don't worry if not. Your tea-table is the star
attraction, so your main aim is to make the rest of the room
a simple and elegant backdrop for that centrepiece.*

TOP TIP

• • • • • • • • • • • • • • • •

Check out charity shops for vintage-style cushions to place around the room. Anything lace, crocheted, knitted or floral will look great.

DIM IT SOME...

• • • • • • • • • • • • • • • •

Candles are a great way of creating a gentle atmosphere and a cosy, old-time feel to a room. Invest in some tea lights and find small vases, jam jars, ramekins and tea-cups to put them in (see my ideas on p.24 for inspiration). Be careful though: always put tea lights in a heatproof container and make sure all candles are out before you leave the room. Side lamps also give a warm, intimate feel to a room – look for ones you can bring in from elsewhere in the house, and avoid turning on harsh overhead bulbs if you can.

THROW AWAY!

• •

A few artfully placed cloths and throws over your tables and other large pieces of modern furniture will pretty the room up in no time.

TOP TIP

• • • • • • • • • • • • • • • •

Charity shops often have wonderful embroidered tablecloths too. If not, try a white sheet or even a lace curtain to get that vintage effect!

BEAUTIFUL BUNTING

Nothing gives a room a more vintage feel than bunting and it's so easy to make! You can use just about any material you can find, from wallpaper, wrapping paper – even newspaper – to old clothes.

You will need:
- Fabric or paper
- Scissors
- Card
- Thick ribbon
- Fabric or paper glue
- Pins

1. ....
Carefully cut a triangle shape out of card to use as your bunting template.

2. ....
Draw around your template on to the back of your paper or material (with fabric, draw on the opposite side to where the pattern shows). To keep your template in place, pin it to the material.

3. ....
Carefully cut out your triangles. If you're using material don't worry if it frays a little; it will add to the vintage look!

4. ....
Lay your bunting triangles along the floor or table, then place small blobs of glue along the top of each one. Now, carefully place along the top of each triangle a single length of ribbon to string them together. This can be a bit tricky, so go slowly! (If you have time to do it really neatly and securely, fold the top edge of the bunting triangle over the top of the ribbon, and then glue it on both sides.

5. ....
Wait for the glue to dry, then hang your bunting up!

Hello Kitty's
TOP TIP
....
Make sure you leave enough ribbon at the ends of your bunting, so that you can hang it up.

THE PERFECT FLOWERS

Make your tea party bloom with some fresh flowers! The best (and most affordable) way to do this is to choose flowers that are in season. So check out my chart, then decide which flowers you want to have at your party.

Season	Flowers
Spring	Daffodils, hyacinths, lilies, tulips
Summer	Peonies, lavender, marigolds, roses
Autumn	Gerberas, sunflowers, iris, lisianthuses
Winter	Holly, camellias, mimosa, hydrangea

Hello Kitty's
TOP TIP

Wild flowers look lovely, too. Look in your garden for daisies and dandelions to mix with your bouquets – or just use greenery – super stylish!

MAKE A CORSAGE

A pretty corsage will make any outfit look sweet and totally vintage. You can even make more and hand them out to your guests, if you're feeling generous!

You will need:

- Flowers and leaves
- Scissors
- Elastic band
- Ribbon

1. Pick one or two flowers and a couple of leaves.
2. Carefully snip the stalks of your flowers so they are all the same length. Your whole corsage should be about 10cm long. Then pop an elastic band around the stalks to keep them together.
3. Wind ribbon around the bottom of your arrangement to make it look pretty!

Hello Kitty's
TOP TIP

Attach your corsage to your outfit using a safety pin, or use more ribbon to tie it to your wrist.

TOTALLY TEACUPS

It always seems that tea tastes better when it's served in a pretty teacup. But have you ever thought that teacups can make cute decorations, too?

FLOWER POWER

Take some fresh flowers and cut the stems low so that they fit into your teacup without falling out. Add a little water to your teacup to keep your flowers fresh. So sweet!

SNACK TIME

Fill your teacups with sweets, nuts or fruit to make gorgeous and unusual snack holders!

CUTE CANDLE

These will look great on your tea party table. You can buy them ready-made, or make them using old teacups.

1. Place a length of string (you can use special candlewick string if you have it) into a teacup and hold it upright with a pair of chopsticks, taped at each end.
2. Warm some wax crystals in a saucepan until melted, then pour it into the teacup. Make sure there is some string left at the top.
3. Add some perfumed oil if you want a scented candle – just don't make it too strong!
4. Wait for the wax to cool, then place on your tea party table ready to light.

DESIGN A CAKE STAND

Create your own vintage-style cake stand with plates and tea cups (mugs will do if you have nothing else to hand). Place one cup upside down in the centre of a large dinner plate. Balance another plate on top (a slightly smaller plate is ideal). Use adhesive putty or double-sided tape to secure. Add another teacup-and-plate layer if it looks safe enough!

Hello Kitty's
TOP TIP

Why not make place names for your guests too, using some of the motifs from the invitation designs on p.13

FABULOUS FASHION

A party is always a great excuse for getting dressed up – and never more so than a vintage-style tea. Although informal and fun, in the old days a tea party's guests would have taken great care with their clothes, hair, nails and make-up. It's a great excuse to go as frilly and fancy as you like!

DRESS IT UP

A tea party is the perfect opportunity to wear a 'tea dress' – which really just means a pretty, usually knee-length, dress that you feel comfortable in. You can dress it up with hats, heels, and hair-dos, or down with loose hair and no accessories – it's up to you. If it's chilly, pair with a little cardigan.

JEWELS

Brooches are oh-so-very vintage, and they're a great thing to pick up inexpensively in charity shops and jumble sales. They come in all shapes, sizes and styles – my favourite kind are flowers. Beads are gorgeous too and give any outfit a vintage feel.

Hello Kitty's
TOP TIP

Add a bow à la Hello Kitty for an instant dash of retro glamour!

FASCINATING HATS

Team your pretty dress with a fancy little hat with a veil – you could even make your own! Round woven discs are available online or from good haberdashers and veil netting is easy to buy from any fabric shop, or just customise a hat you already have. You can cover it with fabric, or decorate it with buttons, brooches, beads, feathers – anything you like – and pin it to your hair using hair grips.

AMAZING ACCESSORIES

If a hat feels like too much, why not simply decorate your hair with a flower tucked behind your ear, a feather, a cute hair grip or a Hello Kitty bow? Turn the page for some fab vintage hairstyles to finish your look.

HERITAGE HAIR-DOS

A vintage hair-do is a fab way to finish off a retro outfit. There are very simple ways to give your hair an old-time touch – check out these sweet ideas!

PARTING WAYS

Simply trying a new parting is one way of instantly changing your look. A deep side-parting harks back to hairstyles from the 1930s, 40s and 50s – the heyday of the vintage look.

Here's how to get it:

1. Brush your hair back, away from your head.
2. Place the edge of a comb on a point about 3cm from your centre parting, on whichever side feels most comfortable.
3. Draw the comb back along your head in a straight line. Experiment with how far from the centre you can go.
4. Pin your side parting in place with hair grips and – ta da!

VICTORY ROLLS

So-called because this was one of the favourite hairstyles during WWII, this hair-do takes a bit of mastering, but the results are well worth it!

1. Separate hair down the middle forming two sections (as if you were doing pigtails). Starting on one side of your head, take the front section towards the top of your head. Repeat on the other side, making sure you have exactly the same sections of hair on each side.

2. Twist the end of one side section at the end so you can hold it between thumb and forefinger, then wrap it loosely around two fingers and begin rolling in toward the scalp.

3. Roll all the way to the scalp so you have a hollow roll, and pin in place on your scalp with hair grips.

4. Repeat with the separated section of hair on the other side.

CHEEKY CHEAT

If this is too complicated you can get a version of the look by pulling the hair that would be in a fringe forward in front of your face. Twist it several times almost up to your scalp, and then pin it back with Kirby grips into a sort of twisted quiff.

Hello Kitty's
TOP TIP

Wetting the ends of your hair will help you to keep control of it while rolling. You can add a scarf to complete this look whether you wear it up or down.

The Home Spa Party

Whether it's trying out a new hair-do, decorating your nails, or just snuggling up in your dressing gown and slippers to enjoy a gossip, Hello Kitty thinks a home spa is even more relaxed and fun than the real thing! Why not combine your home spa with a DVD and sleepover – by the end of all this pampering, your guests are bound to be too relaxed to move anyway! ZZzzzzz…

Hello Kitty's Head Massage

A head massage is just heaven. It sweeps away tension and stress that you may be holding in your muscles without realising and makes you feel great all over!

1.

Stand behind the person to be massaged, with your hands resting lightly on their shoulders. Make sure their hair is loose and untied.

2.

Now as if you were gently kneading dough, squeeze the muscle on each side of the neck from the base of the neck out towards each shoulder. You're gradually warming it up – lightly at first and then harder, pushing any tightness away and off the ends of the shoulders.

3. Next, pressing with your thumbs at the base of the neck, make small circular movements on either side of the spine.

4. Continue this movement up towards the hairline, then work your way out to each shoulder again. Repeat this 3 times.

5. Next, spread your fingers and place on either side of the head as if you were shampooing the hair, with light pressure from the fingers and also the heels of the hands. Work your way like this over the whole head.

6. Now rub the scalp all over more firmly with the heel of your hand. This really gets the blood moving and toxins out!

7. Finish by repeating step 2. If you want to do shorter massages, you can skip some steps – don't skip too many though or you'll regret it when it's your turn!

Hello Kitty's
Top Tip
It helps to stand at the side of the person, supporting their forehead with one hand.

Homemade Beauty

Try these easy recipes for natural loveliness.
Not only can all the ingredients be found in
your cupboards or fridge, but they'll leave
you feeling good enough to eat, too!

BODY SOFTENER

Dry, rough skin on your hands, knees, feet or elbows? This simple mix will have them silky soft in no time!

You will need:

- 1 x tablespoon (tbsp) olive oil
- 1 x teaspoon (tsp) sea salt flakes

Rub the ingredients together with your hands and then massage gently into the area to be treated for about a minute. Wipe clean with a warm flannel for instant smoothness!

(NB: don't try this on your face – the skin is more sensitive there.)

YUMMY FACE MASK

This recipe is full of amazing natural ingredients to leave your skin glowing. Just remember – no nibbling!

You will need:

- 2 x carrots
- 1 tbsp honey
- 1 tbsp olive oil
- a few drops of lemon juice

Wash and chop the carrots, then steam them until they're soft and mash them up with a fork. Stir in the honey and the olive oil, then add a few drops of lemon juice (and a few more if you have greasy skin). Add a little water if needed, until you have a creamy (not runny) paste. Now gently wash your face and pat dry before applying the face mask everywhere but your eyes. Leave it for about 15 minutes, then rinse and pat dry again with a fluffy towel – beautiful!

HONEY & PROTEIN DEEP CONDITIONER

For the softest, healthiest hair imaginable!

You will need:

- 1 tsp honey
- 2 tbsp olive oil
- 1 egg yolk

Combine the egg, honey and olive oil in a bowl and mix well. Massage into your hair, concentrating on the ends and then put on a shower cap and leave on for 30 minutes. Rinse and shampoo for gorgeous glowing locks!

EYES BRIGHT

. . . .

This classic eye treatment will not only make your eyes shiny, but treats the delicate skin around them, too. A great remedy if you've been having too many late nights.

You will need:
- A few cucumber slices
- A soft pillow

Place one slice of cucumber over each closed eye. Lie back, sigh happily and let them do their magic. (It's best to leave them for at least 5 minutes – any longer though, and you might fall asleep!)

LUSCIOUS LASHES

. . . .

Nourish and condition your eyelashes with this wonderful oil from the castor bean – one of beauty's best-kept secrets. It will help your eyelashes to grow thick and long, and stop them breaking by nourishing and conditioning.

You will need:
- an old toothbrush
- castor oil

Simply dip the brush in the oil and comb it through your lashes and brows. It's a great way to define your brows and lashes too instead of wearing mascara – careful not to get it in your eyes, though!

Hello Kitty's
Top Tip

You can get castor oil in many independent chemists or online.

AVOCADO CREAMY FACE & HAIR MASK

The oil from these rich fruits is used in many shop-bought beauty and hair products. Why not get it completely fresh and straight from the source instead?

You will need:

- One avocado!

Peel the avacado, then mash in a bowl, taking care not to spill any of the precious juice!

Add a little milk or olive oil if needed to make a paste. Now massage the pulp through your hair and over your face. If that's too messy, use it all on your hair and rub the inside of the skin over your face instead. Wait for 10 minutes, then wash away and pat dry with a soft towel, leaving your hair and skin feeling baby soft and moisturised.

Hello Kitty's
Top Tip

It's best to use a ripe avocado – choose one that's not rock hard when you give it a gentle squeeze; it should feel soft but not squashy.

Nail It!

Your hands are like a showcase for you! They work hard and are on view all the time, so they deserve the very best treatment. Luckily, there are so many fun ways to make them look pretty!

HAND TREATS

Before you begin, why not give your hands a pamper with the body softener recipe on p.34. Then, try these cuticle-softening tricks to get your hands silky soft, strong and ready for decorating!

NAIL STRENGTHENING SOAK

You will need:
- 2 egg yolks, beaten
- 1/4 cup milk
- 1 tbsp honey

Mix the ingredients in a small bowl. Soak nails for 10-15 minutes. Rinse well. Protein from the eggs and calcium from the milk will make those nails hard as rocks!

CITRUS NAIL GROWTH SOAK

You will need:
• Orange juice (yes, that's all!)
Soak the nails for at least 10 minutes, then rinse. Easy! Orange juice contains folic acid which is great for hair and nail growth.

POLKA DOTS

Why not try painting polka dots in various colours over a contrasting background? Or instead of dots you could paint a Hello Kitty bow on each nail – supercute!

TIPPY-TOPS

What about painting just the tips of your nails with teeny tiny little flowers in a row? So easy and subtle, but really effective! First paint your nail with clear polish, outlining the tip with white French polish. Then, simply paint your flowers on; a dot in the centre and five little dots for petals round the edge of each.

WALL-PEEPERS

Try painting upside-down cute little eyes and foreheads on the end of each nail, as if they're peering over the top of a wall.

Hello Kitty's Top Tip

Try doing something different on each nail for a great mix-and-match look.

Messing with Make-up

*Most of the time I prefer looking natural, but it's fun playing around with make-up and creating different looks – a bit like dressing up! Here are some of my **top tips** to get you looking **tip-top**!*

THE NATURAL LOOK

This is my favourite and it's super-easy to achieve.
- Use a small dab of petroleum jelly on an old toothbrush and comb it through your eyelashes for a really natural mascara look. It's a treat for your lashes too and keeps them silky smooth! Comb it through your eyebrows too for smooth, sleek brows.

- A tiny smear of petroleum jelly on your lips and cheekbones just beneath the eyes will give your skin a healthy sheen and keep it in tip-top condition too.

THE EYE-FLICK

This classic look has appeared on starlets and beauties since Cleopatra's time. It's lasted because it works, lengthening the eye and sweeping up to give a cat-like, mysterious look. Take a brush eyeliner and begin drawing a smooth line, starting near the inside corner of your eye. Continue along the lash-line keeping as close to the lashes as possible. End with a flick at the side going up at a similar angle to your outer eyelashes. This takes a lot of practice, so don't worry if you don't get it first time – especially getting both eyes to match! Keep some cotton buds and a gentle make-up remover close by to correct any errors.

GET LIPPY!

There are so many different lip colours available it can be hard to know where to start, but it's great fun trying them all out to see which suits you. Check out the chart below as a starting point:

Skin tone	Best lipstick colours
Lighter skin tone	light-brown beiges with pink or orange undertones
Olive skin	brownish reds, light browns and raisin shades of lipstick
Dark skin	plums, wines and deep reds

Hello Kitty's Top Tip

Dab a little lip colour on to the end of your finger and rub it on the apples of your cheeks as an easy cream blusher!

The Sass & Style Party

Hello Kitty *adores* fashion – she knows that throwing a style party is a great place to start playing around with your image. Not only is it really fun, but you get valuable feedback on all your efforts, not to mention a little help from your friends! So get out your full-length mirror, put on some catwalk tunes and get ready to find *your* style!

SUSS YOUR STYLE

The world of fashion can seem overwhelming – there are so many clothes in the shops and they change all the time! Where do you even begin? Why not start with a group of friends, a big pile of fashion magazines and a pair of scissors?

You will need:

- Some A3 card
- Scissors (several pairs)
- A big pile of fashion magazines (tell everyone to bring some with them)
- Adhesive putty

1. ....

All the top fashion stylists are used to making a 'look book' (sometimes known as a 'mood board') – and it's super-easy to do! First, make yourselves a nice cup of tea (or make one of my delicious drinks on p.134). Now, grab a few fashion magazines and start to flick your way through them. Every time you see something that you like, STOP. Cut it out. Now keep flicking. See? It's easy!

2. ●●●●●●●●●●●●●●●●●●●●●●●●●●●●

When everyone has cut out as many bags, skirts, shoes, hairstyles, lip colours, earrings, coats, dresses, scarves and belts as they want (plus anything else that takes their fancy), then STOP again. Have a biscuit.

3. ●●●●●●●●●●●●●●●●●●●●●●●●●●●●

Now, in no particular order, stick everything on to your large piece of paper or card; the bigger the better so that you can keep adding to it. Use adhesive putty so that you can take pictures off and move them around if you want to try them somewhere else. You might want to put outfits together, but don't feel you have to at all because then you may get stuck. Just put it all together in a kind of jumble or theme it by colour or style.

4. ●●●●●●●●●●●●●●●●●●●●●●●●●●●●

Stand your mood board somewhere where you'll see it all the time. Regularly seeing images of the kinds of fabrics and shapes that appeal to you will help you recognise your style when you're shopping, rather than just feeling bewildered by the choice.

Hello Kitty's
TOP TIP
●●●●●●●●●●●●●●●●●●●●
If two of you want the same picture, then no fighting! Mark it up to be photocopied next time you're near a colour copier!

SWISHY SWAPPY!

Hello Kitty knows most of you have heard about recycling (and if you haven't, take out those headphones!). It's a great way of making sure things don't get wasted, which is good news for the environment and sends out the message that we don't want fast fashion at any cost – double-good! Swishing may sound a little strange, but it's just the latest word for swapping: recycling your clothes by giving away unwanted items and getting something new and rather fabulous in return! It's a brilliant thing to do at a party, though there are a few ground rules that everyone should remember to make sure it doesn't turn into a rugby match!

- Before the party, dig out as many mirrors as you can from around the house – at least one full length, and ideally a couple of hand-held ones too so people can view themselves from behind. Everyone will be wanting to see how they look at once, so the more, the better.

- Make sure you have enough coat hangers (you can ask people to bring their own). If you've got one, a portable clothes rack is a great way to display the clothes; otherwise hang them around the room – on the back of the door; on a picture rail and on the window sills.

- Everyone should try on the clothes they like the look of first and make a note of the ones that they would like. Then, when you've all finished trying things on, you can hold them up one at a time and hand them out! If more than one person wants the same item, make them raffle tickets (draw two 1's on a piece of paper – give one to the first person and put the other in the hat. Repeat with 2; 3 and so on for the remaining contestants) – and have a lucky draw!

Hello Kitty's
TOP TIP
Swishing is a great, no-risk way of trying out clothes you might never normally think of wearing!

SASS & STYLE

iPATCH!

Hello Kitty adores patches – they're so cute and pretty! Sometimes she sews them on to her clothes even when there's no hole to cover! Her favourite patches are in pretty fabrics with small prints on them that clash with the item she is sewing them on to.

How to sew on a patch:

1. First, copy the template opposite on to a piece of plain card. If you need your patch to be bigger, simply add the same length on to each end of each line with a ruler and use the card template to make sure the angles are correct.

48

TEMPLATE

the cloth and through the edge of the patch. Try to keep the stitches small and straight as you go round.

3. ••••••••••••••••••••••••••••

For a neater look, you can turn the edges of your patch under by 0.5-1cm all the way round. Iron the edges, then sew along the folds – you can do this from between the garment and the underside of the patch most of the way round, but will need to finish the last couple of sides from the top side so make your stitches as small and as neat as possible!

2. ••••••••••••••••••••••••••••

Next, place your patch right side up exactly where you want it to go, and pin it around the edges to keep it in place. Now, turn your garment inside out. Thread a needle, and make the thread double thickness by tying the two loose ends together at the end. Time to sew! Following the line of the pins, begin to sew small stitches, in and out of

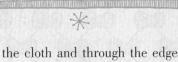

Hello Kitty's
TOP TIP
••••••••••••••
Great places to put patches: on the elbows of any top or jumper; on bags; where you might usually wear a brooch – just about anywhere, in fact!

49

BUTTON BAZAAR

Hello Kitty loves collecting buttons! Most people seem to have a button collection of some sort – if your friends don't, they can pick them up in fabric shops or the haberdashery section of big department stores, or find great vintage ones in second-hand shops, markets and fairs. Get everyone to bring their buttons to your style party and mix and match!

ALL CHANGE!

Buttons are great for transforming clothes. They can completely change the look of a piece, and are a great way of decorating a plain, boring old shirt or cardigan. Buttons can make or break an item – cheap, plastic buttons really let clothes down, but you can make an inexpensive piece of clothing look a million dollars with a smart set of buttons!

Contrasting colours or styles can look great – a set of little shaped duck/sailing boat buttons on a shirt can look so cute, or little red hearts on a brown cardie – adorable! Plus it's so fun trying out what works with what. And they don't take long to sew on, so if you decide you want a change, just snip them off and start again!

Hello Kitty's
TOP TIP
You can pick up great old military brass buttons or sailor buttons at vintage fairs or in second-hand shops

DECORATIONS

Buttons just look fab, without having to serve as fasteners. Try sewing little clusters on to a plain bag – maybe in the shape of a flower or heart. They also make great 'trims'. Sew a row of them along a length of ribbon, before attaching to the bottom of a pair of curtains, around the opening edge of a bag (see p.60), or around the cover of a book (see p.54).

JEWELLERY

Buttons can also look fab as a bracelet, necklace, brooch or even a pair of earrings. Craft shops sell brooch and earring backs and all you need to do is glue your button on (use a strong, even super, glue for this to make sure it sticks).

The Crafty Party

There's nothing more satisfying than making something with your own hands, as any granny will tell you. Whether you want to decorate your bedroom, make your own jewellery or create a unique gift for someone, Hello Kitty has loads of simple but effective ideas in this section. And it's a great thing to do in a group because if you get stuck, your friends are on hand to help you out!

It's A Cover-up

Try covering up plain, boring textbooks with this fab and simple technique – covered books make your shelves and bag look so pretty! It's great for using up scraps of material that you can't find another use for, or leftover wall paper – good-quality wrapping paper works well too. Careful though – once you've got the covering bug, no book will be safe!

You will need:
- Paper or fabric
- Suitable glue
- A book
- Scissors

1. ....

Place your book cover down and open on to the underside of your paper or fabric.

BOOK
PAGE 1

2. ••••••••••••••••••••••••••••••
Trace around the edge. Make sure you get the width of the spine correct as this will affect how the book opens and closes.

3. ••••••••••••••••••••••••••••••
Add your 'flaps' (see diagram) – make sure these are at least 2cm deep.

4. ••••••••••••••••••••••••••••••
Cut out your template and place the book over it. Glue the front cover first, then the back – make sure you smooth out any wrinkles, then stick down your folds.

5. ••••••••••••••••••••••••••••••
Just tuck the extra bits above the spine down so that they are not visible. Hey presto – a beautiful, mysterious new book!

DECORATIVE COVERS
••••••••••••••••••••••••••••••

If you have some scrap paper or material that you love, but it's not big enough to cover the whole book, no problem! Cover your book in plain brown parcel paper (you can get it from any Post Office or stationers). Then add your smaller paper in a band around the middle, or in a 'patch' at a jaunty angle, as decoration. You could also cut out pretty shapes – what about stars out of yellow coloured paper or red hearts?

Hello Kitty's
Top Tip
••••••••••••••••
Covered books make great personal gifts. Cover an inexpensive diary, address book or notebook and finish it off with a neat little ribbon tied in a bow.

Craft it

Puff Party

*These simple little fabric rounds look great –
and they're sew easy to make! You can do as
few or as many as you like, and the ways
you can use them are endless!*

1. ....

Cut out a circle of card to use as a template and then draw around it on to your fabric. Make it as large as you like – just remember, your final puff will be half this size.

2. ....

Using a needle and doubled-up thread, fold over a small hem of about 1cm and stitch all the way around the edge of your

56

circle, going in and out with the needle. Make your stitches quite small – about 3mm each. Start and finish sewing with your thread on the 'right' side (not the one with the hem).

3. ....
When you reach the end, leave long ends of thread. Tie them in a single knot first and then…

4. ....
…pull them! Help the fabric along them by gathering up the folds with your fingers and pushing them along the thread. When the fabric is all gathered equally, tie the threads up in a double knot and snip. Well done! You've just made your first Pretty Puff!

PUFF PERFECT

....

You can use your puffs for so many things! Decorate a bag or top (or what about a little hat for your vintage tea-party? See p.27). Make more puffs using the same material or different fabrics for a patchwork effect. You can stitch them all together in a row to make a necklace, bracelet, curtain tie-backs for your bedroom or to trim a lampshade. Or attach them to ring-bases or earring backs (available from crafting shops) to make your own jewellery. Or, if you're on a roll, stitch lots of rows together to make a scarf, blanket or throw! And of course, all of these items make gorgeous gifts – flip the page to see how to make beautiful bags and boxes to put them in!

Craft it

Gorgeous Gift-holders

Getting a little gift bag or box is so exciting – but they can sometimes cost almost as much as the gift itself! Use the two templates opposite to make your own beautiful boxes and bags to present your... presents! (If you had time, you could even make enough for all the guests at your party and pop in a little cake as a leaving gift!)

You will need:

- Scissors
- Glue
- Card (thick enough to feel strong but not so thick that it won't fold!)
- Paper to cover the card. Or simply use coloured card and decorate it yourself with

pictures, stamps, glitter etc. Remember sometimes less is more – a small written message such as 'Thank you' on each side looks very elegant! Or why not trace over Hello Kitty's face to give your box a special theme?

Hello Kitty's
Top Tip
....

You can change the measurements to
make these as big or as small as you like
to fit your gift – just make sure you make
the same changes everywhere...

Hello Kitty's Odds and Bobs

There are so many fun, cute and simple things you can do to transform your home or wardrobe. Get your friends over to try some of these fab ideas out!

RAISE THE CURTAIN

Make simple curtain tie-backs in matching fabric – or jazz them up with contrasting colours and patterns (floral/striped tie-backs look great with plain curtains and vice versa!)

Here's how:

1. Take two long strips of material of equal length and width – long enough to go around the bulk of your curtains and then hang down (or whatever you want them to do). Make the width wider by about 1cm than you want the final width to be.
2. Place them on top of one another with the topsides facing in and the two undersides facing out. Starting at one end, about 0.5cm

in from both edges, begin to stitch down one side. Keep your line straight and don't make the stitches too small or tight. At the end, continue around and go back down the other side.

3. About 0.5cm from the end of the second length, tie a knot in your thread and then turn your material 'sock' inside out. Tuck the remaining edges of the last width under and sew neatly together.

4. Now press with an iron. Congratulations – that's one tie-back! Only one to go!

ARE BAGS YOUR BAG?

Make yourself a pretty fabric purse! Choose a material that isn't too flimsy – denim's a great one to use. Double it over so you have two layers and pin them together. Now, from the fold (which will form the bottom of your bag) cut through both layers, the square or rectangular shape you'd like your bag to be. Make it about 1cm larger than the final size all the way round. Now follow instruction 2 in the curtain tie-backs section, except when you reach the fourth and final side of your bag (the opening), turn the rough edges over as hems and stitch them to their own side, not together. Now sew a handle of whatever length you like with ribbon or braid – stitch the ends to the inside of your bag.

Hello Kitty's
Top Tip

Why not decorate your bag with buttons or a pretty puff (see p.56) to give it a stylish, individual look?

The Games & Giggles Party

It doesn't matter what your age, you're never too old to enjoy playing games! It's a sure-fire way to get a party going, and will get even the most timid of your friends out of their shell. It may be a good idea to have some small prizes such as a bowl of sweets on hand for the winner (and to cheer up the losers!). Now – let the games begin!

Memory Madness

Hello Kitty guarantees this game will get your guests thinking fast, racking their brains and giggling lots!

What to do:
Before your guests arrive, arrange some items on to a tray and cover them with a tea towel. Make sure none of the items can be seen when you cover your tray.

You can use whatever you like, but make sure you have a mix of big and small items. Here's a list of ideas to get you thinking!

- Teacup
- Safety pin
- Jewellery
- Notepad and pen
- Mobile phone
- Spoon
- Photograph
- Toothbrush
- Hair clips

How to play:

1. ....
   Give each guest a pen and a piece of paper.

2. ....
   Place the tray in the middle of your room and tell each guest that they have 10 seconds from the moment you lift the tea towel to look at the tray and memorise everything that is on it.

3. ....
   After 10 seconds, quickly cover the tray and make sure none of the items can be seen – we don't want any cheating!

Hello Kitty's
Top Tip
Try and find something really silly to put on the tray, like a half eaten apple or a funny photograph!

4. ....
   Your guests now have half a minute to write down as many of the items as they can. The person who remembers the most is the winner!

Hello Kitty's
Top Tip
If there is a tie for first place, ask your friends to spell tea tray backwards – the person who does it quickest is the winner!

Fun & games

Teapotty Doodles

This head-scribbling game is perfect for artistic friends – it's also a fun one to play if you're having an Alice in Wonderland themed party – see p.84.

What to do:

Get some plain white paper plates, one per guest, and felt-tip pens. It's also handy to have a picture of a teapot to hand, or to place a teapot so everyone can see it.

How to play:

1. Give each guest a paper plate and a pen.

2. Ask each friend to place the paper plate on top of their heads.

3. Now ask them to draw the shape of a teapot on to the paper plate while it's still on top of their heads!

4. The person who draws the best teapot is the winner.

Hello Kitty's
Top Tip

If your friends like the game, have two or three rounds drawing different objects.

Puddle Pranks

This game is great fun, especially with the 'twist' at the end. (Though it's a good idea to choose someone who can laugh at themselves for that bit!)

What to do:

1. Lay the paper plates randomly all over the floor, allowing enough space between each plate for a person to stand in. These plates are the 'puddles' that must be avoided. If you stand on one, you're out.
2. Now choose who'll be 'it' first.

How to play:

1. Explain the rules to the player, and allow them to view the puddle pandemonium ahead of them for ten seconds so they can memorise where they all are.
2. Next, blindfold the player, and turn them around three times.
3. Now, set them in the right direction, and see whether they can make their way through the puddles safely!

The twist:

Blindfold a player, then quietly remove all the plates and watch them tiptoe across an empty floor. Naughty, but funny!

Consequences

Get your friends in fits of giggles with this
funny game – it gets seriously silly!

What to do:

Give each of your guests a pen or pencil and a photocopy of the page opposite (or they could all rewrite the headings on A4 sheets of paper).

How to play:

1. Ask each player to fill in the first section of the paper.

2. Now tell everyone to fold their section over and hand it to the person on their right.

3. The next person fills in the following section, then you all repeat step 2.

(TIP: for the boy's name or girl's name, it's always funnier if it's someone you all know – perhaps a friend or someone famous.)

4. When all the sections are filled, everyone should pass their completed papers to the person on their right. Now take it in turns to read them out!

Hello Kitty's
Top Tip
....

Play a drawing version of this game: the first person draws a head and folds it over; the next does the neck, then body and so on.

One day,

Adjective (describing word, like 'lovely', 'smelly', 'difficult' etc)
....

Boy's name
....

...met...

Another adjective
....

Girl's name
....

Where they met (e.g. in a dustbin)
....

He wore
....

She wore
....

He said to her
....

She said to him
....

What the consequence was (the result or outcome)
....

Treasure Hunt

Treasure hunts are such fun and can be as easy or as complicated as you want! There are different ways to go about setting up a great treasure hunt.

CLUES

The main aim is to get your treasure-seekers to move from one spot to another, finding the treasure at the end. You can do this around your party venue, or why not try outside if the weather is good? If you're staying indoors, make sure the clues could be guessed by guests who aren't familiar with your house.

- If you're feeling inspired, it's fun to write the clues in riddles or rhyme

Climb up me; go down me;
on carpet or wood;
the next clue is under me –
if you find it, you're good!

Answer: under the stairs.

- Or, depending on your artistic skills, you could draw a picture or take a close-up photo of where the next clue could be found!

PUZZLES

- Hide pieces of a treasure map around the room for people to find and put together to find the location of the hidden treasure!
- Or, each clue could be a mini home-made jigsaw puzzle, which, when put together simply says the location of the next clue.
- Hold a 'Hello Kitty Baker's Hunt'! Each part of the puzzle could be an ingredient or instruction step for a recipe. Once the whole recipe has been discovered, your guests could go about making it! If you have two competing teams, you could give them a time limit or hold a 'bake-off' judging competition to decide on the winners. (If you want to add yet another level of competition, measure out the ingredients for each recipe beforehand into small sealed containers or bags, and hide them around a different room too, to be found once the recipe has been discovered!)

Hello Kitty's
Top Tip
Don't forget the treasure at the end. A little bag or box of sweets is a great idea, especially for a team, so everyone can share.

HOLLYWOOD   Film Club

PRODUCTION   Hello Kitty

DIRECTOR   3

CAMERA   SCEN

THE CHATTING PARTY

There's nothing like a good natter with your friends
and having a topic to discuss is a great way to get
things started, especially if not all of your guests know
each other well. It can be relaxed and informal – if the
conversation goes off-topic for a while and you find
yourselves chatting about your favourite cupcake flavour,
it doesn't matter – you're all here to have fun, after all!

THE BOOK CLUB

A book club is the perfect choice of party if you love reading. You can do it as a one-off, or make it a regular get-together!

BE PREPARED

You'll need to choose the book well in advance since everyone needs to read it before the party. Try not to choose something that the library only has one copy of, or it could take months to get read!

Make sure most of your guests have agreed on the book – it needs to be something they're prepared to read. The best conversation is usually when some people loved it and some hated it, so try not to go for something too 'safe'.

While reading the book yourself, make notes on the bits you like and don't like so much. Remember everyone's opinion is valid, so don't be shy!

GET THE BALL ROLLING...

Here are some example questions that you may want to think about.

- Were there particular themes that the author kept coming back to? Do you agree with their views?
- Did the book make you think differently about something or become aware of something that perhaps you'd never thought of before?
- Did you relate to the characters in the book? Even if you didn't like them, did they seem realistic?
- How do you think you would have responded to the situations the characters find themselves in?
- Did the book affect you emotionally, such as making

you cry or offending you? Why?
- Do you think it's possible to find a book interesting without actually enjoying it?
- Do you think the book's cover reflected the insides well? What about the blurb on the back?

Chatting

THE FILM CLUB

In some ways, holding a film club is easier than a book club, because it takes very little preparation. You can all actually watch the film together and then discuss it straight after when it's fresh in your minds. Plus there's popcorn…

Chatting

AND… ACTION!

Here are some ideas to get you started on your film club party.

- Try to get a film that everyone will want to watch; it might be a good idea to put three suggestions on your invitation and ask guests to tick their favourite choice when they return their RSVP.

- Make sure you have a seat for everyone, or at least cushions if some people have to sit on the floor (though try not to invite so many people that this happens). If some guests have less comfortable seats, perhaps arrange for them to swap halfway through.

- Take the role of leader to steer the conversation smoothly.

You could use some of the discussion starters from the Book Club on p.74, or print off some reviews before the party – always useful if opinions begin to run dry!

MAKE YOUR OWN POPCORN

....

You will need:
- A large pan with a heavy base
- Popcorn kernels
- Grapeseed oil
- Sugar / butter / golden syrup / maple syrup / salt – to taste

What to do:
1. Put 2 tbsp of oil into the bottom of the pan and turn on the heat at a medium temperature.
2. Pour the kernels into the pan until the base is covered with one layer of kernels. Cover with a lid. Now wait...
3. Soon, you should hear a pop, and then another and then lots!

Stay near the pan now as things will start to happen quickly. Give the pan a shake once or twice during the popping to make sure nothing sticks to the bottom. Make sure you keep the lid on all the time!

4. When you're fairly sure you've heard the final pop, turn the heat off and carefully lift the lid.
5. Now add whichever of the flavourings listed above take your fancy. I like mixing salt and sweet popcorn together – yummy!

POP

THE DISCUSSION CLUB

Got a burning issue you feel strongly about? Maybe it's what's happening to the environment; animal rights; feminism or care of the elderly? It's not often you'll have a chance to rant about it without people edging away from you nervously, but what better place to vent your feelings than over some delicious cakes with your friends?

Hello Kitty's
Top Tip
. . . .
It's worth having an internet connection during the party, so you can look up any information you need.

DO YOUR RESEARCH
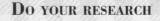

Find out what facts you can about the issue in question before the party. Read articles about it and make notes on important numbers, facts, how you feel and your thoughts.

On the invitation, let your friends know to think of their own topics (if they want) so they can prepare too.

DOWN WITH BAD THINGS!

Follow my leader

It's a good idea, as the host, for you to take the role of 'leader', starting off the discussion in case your pals are feeling timid. Ask questions of the group to get people going, and gently interrupt people who are talking so much that no one else can get a word in edgeways!

- Don't worry if conversation goes off-topic for a while. The point is to have fun and get people sharing thoughts and ideas, after all!
- At the end though, it's a good idea to ask whether anyone had something to say that they didn't get a chance to.
- Feelings can run high when people talk about subjects close to their heart so if things get heated, step in with a nice cool drink and some home-made biscuits.

Get active!

Your Discussion Club may make you want to make changes for the better on any issues you feel strongly about. A quick search on any internet search engine will give you lots of websites for charities and organisations working in the area you're interested in. They can give you lots more information about how to join in and get involved!

HOORAY FOR HELLO KITTY!

THE THEME PARTY

Giving your party a focus can pull an event together and make decisions easier. Throwing a Queen for the Day party? Suddenly everyone has a better idea about what to wear (something suitable for a palace); your food can have a right royal twist and people can behave in a very regal manner. And for the music? What else, but… Queen? Don't stop me now, I'm having such a good time…!

QUEEN FOR THE DAY!

It's always fun to pretend you are royalty!
Celebrate with your subjects and these cute ideas!

CROWNING GLORY

Give your party a regal theme with a sparkling crown on everything. Use this template to add a crown to your bunting, party bags and place names!

YOUR MAJESTY!

Give all your friends fancy noble titles like Duchess, Lady, Countess and Princess. You can add them to their place names and ask everyone to use their 'royal' names at the party.

ROYAL GAMES

Give some of the best traditional party games a regal twist – what about Musical Thrones or Right Royal Musical Statues to get things started? Another fun one is Queenie, Queenie. Choose a player to be the 'Knave' and ask them to stand away from the group while the rest of you secretly decide who will be the Queen. The Queen is given a small ball (a tennis ball is perfect) to hide behind her back. The Queen and her subjects line up with their hands behind their backs facing the Knave. The Knave has to run through the line and try to spot who is the Queen, while the players all try to keep their backs turned. If the Queen is spotted, the Knave gets a reward and gets to sit down; the Queen then becomes the Knave and the game starts again!

ALL THAT GLITTERS

Using gold and silver gives an instant royal feel to your party. Sprinkle glitter on your table, pop chocolate coins in your party bags and make sure you serve the glittering fruit punch from p.144. Label all your food with royal names such as 'Princess Punch' or 'Quivering Queen's Jelly'.

THEMED

WELCOME TO WONDERLAND!

An Alice in Wonderland theme creates a tea party fit for a mad hatter!

PLAYING CARDS

Playing cards are a really cool way of making your party instantly Alice. You can use a playing card for each guest as a place name by writing their name on the back; string them together to use as bunting or simply scatter them over the table as decoration.

TEAPOT SURPRISE

Teapots are totally Alice, so gather together as many as you can to use as table decorations. You could fill them with flowers to make madcap vases or perhaps use them as unusual serving bowls for all the delicious things you'll be baking from the recipe section! Why not use them to serve an unexpected drink (soft drinks rather than tea!) or just pop a random item inside to give your guests a funny surprise. The more bonkers, the better!

EAT ME, DRINK ME!

Why not make little labels like these to add to your drinks and food.

MAD HAT CAPERS

Ask each of your guests to bring a hat with them – top hats are perfect but anything will do. During the party, line the hats up in a row and get your guests to stand behind a marker at a distance from them. Everyone has to take it in turns to throw in a beanbag (or toy dormouse if you have one!). Keep score to see who manages to get the mouse in a hat the most times!

DRINK ME

EAT ME

SPRING HAS SPRUNG!

As the weather turns warmer, I like nothing better than getting outdoors and setting up my own spring-themed tea party.

EGGS-ELLENT

Make cute egg decorations! Boil them until they're hard, then paint and decorate your eggs any way you like! Put your guests' names on them to use as place names, dot them around the table, hang them from tree branches out in the garden, or put them in a vase indoors.

BLOOMING LOVELY

Nothing says spring better than pretty blossoms. Fresh flowers are lovely, but you can get the effect by cutting flower shapes out of pretty paper to use as decorations, too. Add them to your invitations, party bags and table settings.

TISSUE ROSES

You will need:
- Tissue paper (like toilet roll)
- Thread

What to do:
1. Take two sections of plain tissue paper and place them one on top of the other.
2. Fold the top over about 1cm deep. Now fold it back on itself and then forwards again, gradually making a concertina or fan effect.
3. When you have folded your paper backwards and forwards to the end, press the folded length in half and tie it with a piece of thread in a double knot.
4. Now, being careful, find the topmost sheet of tissue paper on one side and peel it away from the layers below, towards the tied centre. Do the same with all the layers beneath, and repeat on the other side until – ta-da! You've made a paper rose!
5. You can scatter your roses on the picnic blanket, or tie them to nearby branches to make them look blooming!

SPRING TREASURE HUNT

This game is perfect to play in a garden or park. Give each guest a list and a pencil, then give them a set time to be back at the starting point (half an hour works well). The person who has collected the most items from their list is the winner. Use these ideas, or come up with your own!
- A leaf with a hole in it
- A petal
- Two rocks or pebbles the same size
- Something rough
- Something smooth
- A leaf bigger than your hand
- A daisy

THEMED

MERRY CHRISTMAS!

Who doesn't love Christmas?
It's the perfect time of year to
host a festive tea party!

RED, GOLD AND GREEN

These colours are perfect to give your party a festive feel. Theme your party table around these colours, with paper plates, ribbon and table confetti.

WRAPPING PAPER BUNTING

Once you've wrapped all your gifts, keep hold of any leftover wrapping paper. Flip back to p.20 and follow the directions to create some truly Christmassy decorations!

SING!

Christmas songs are so much fun to sing! Choose your favourites and write or print out the words to hand out to your guests. You can either sing along to a recording, or just let your voices do the work!

THEMED

CHRISTMAS WREATH CRISPIES

These super-cute treats are perfect yuletide yumminess!

You will need:

- 100g butter/margarine
- 100g marshmallows
- 200g crisped rice cereal
- Green food colouring
- Red icing pen

1. Carefully melt the butter and marshmallows in a pan, then pour the mixture into a large bowl.
2. Next, add your rice cereal, a few handfuls at a time, and mix well.
3. Now it's time to turn your crispy cakes green! Add a few drops of food colouring at a time until you get the colour you want. Remember: you can always add more, but you can't take away – so be careful!
4. The next step is a bit messy, so you might want to cover your table or work surface in paper! When the mixture is cold, take a handful and create a ball. Place your ball on a plate and flatten it so it's about 2cm thick. Finally, make a hole in the middle of the crispy cake to make a wreath shape.
5. For a final touch, use your red icing pen to make little berries and a bow at the bottom.

THE
RECIPES

Baking Mad!

Cooking is so much fun, but it helps to be prepared before you start. That way, your baking will be... a piece of cake!

GENERAL EQUIPMENT

Check through the list opposite before you begin your baking session. It's useful to have the basics, but if anything is missing, don't panic! None of these recipes should require any very specialist kitchen equipment, and there's bound to be a recipe to suit what you already have.

- An apron
- A mixing bowl or two
- Wooden spoon, metal spoon, spatula, whisk
- Weighing scales
- Measuring spoons (or a tablespoon and teaspoon)
- Rolling pin

THE PROOF IS IN THE PUDDING!

Getting the right amount of ingredients is really important. Baking is a science as well as an art. Read the ingredients list and carefully measure out everything you need beforehand, to check you have enough.

HELLO KITTY'S
TOP TIP

Read a recipe all the way through before you begin. That way you won't get any surprises!

HEALTH AND SAFETY

Wash your hands thoroughly before you begin touching ingredients. Always wash your hands after handling any raw meat or fish. Be careful when dealing with a hot oven, too. Always wear oven gloves when handling anything hot. Don't touch anything electrical with wet hands. And no licking the spoon until the end!

IF AT FIRST YOU DON'T SUCCEED...

Practice makes perfect! It's a good idea to try your recipe before the party – not everything comes out right first time, so don't worry if your recipes don't look exactly like the pictures. Remember that they are your version of the recipe, so don't be afraid to decorate them however you like and make them your own!

Brilliant Brioche Buns

Nothing beats the taste of freshly-baked bread
– and these buns smell heavenly too.

Ingredients:

(makes around 9 buns)

- 15ml warm milk
- 1 x 7g sachet of active dry yeast
- 35g sugar
- 2 large eggs
- 425g strong white bread flour
- 55g plain flour
- 1 teaspoon salt
- 35g unsalted butter, softened
- Sesame seeds (optional)

You will need:

- Measuring jug
- Glass bowl
- Mixing bowl
- Plastic wrap
- Baking sheet
- Shallow oven-proof pan

1. ....

In a glass bowl, mix 240ml of warm water, the milk, yeast and sugar. Let it stand for about 10 minutes until it looks foamy – magic! Meanwhile, beat one egg with a fork.

2. ....
In a large bowl, mix the flours together with the salt, then add the butter and rub into the flour between your fingers, making crumbs. Next, stir in the yeast mixture and 1 beaten egg until you have a dough. Scrape the dough on to a clean, well-floured counter and knead, scooping it up, slapping it on the counter and turning it, until it becomes smooth and elastic (this takes about ten minutes). The dough will be on the sticky side so it can be a bit messy, but keep in mind that the more flour you knead in, the tougher the buns will get.

3. ....
Shape the dough into a ball and return it to the bowl. Cover the bowl with plastic wrap and leave it in a warm place until it has doubled in size – magic again! (This should take one to two hours.)

4. ....
Line a baking sheet with lightly greased and floured parchment paper. Now divide the dough into 8 equal parts. Gently roll each into a ball and arrange two to three inches apart on the baking sheet. Again, let the buns rise in a warm place for one to two hours.

5. ....
Set a large shallow pan of water on the floor of the oven and make sure the rack is on the middle shelf. Preheat the oven to 200°C/Gas Mark 6.

6. ....
Beat the remaining egg with one tablespoon of water and brush some on top of buns. Sprinkle with sesame seeds. Now put it in the oven, turning the baking tray halfway through baking, until the tops of the buns are golden brown (about 15 minutes).

Pizza Stars

These cute little pizza-bites are super-simple but super-fun!

Ingredients:
- Sliced bread (white or brown)
- Star-shaped cookie cutter (any shape is fine, really)
- Butter
- Tomato paste
- Grated cheddar cheese

Optional toppings:
- Diced salami or ham
- Sliced peppers
- Mushrooms
- Goats cheese
- Sliced olives

1. ....
   First, cut as many whole shapes out of one piece of bread as you can, and when you have as many as you need, place them under the grill until they are lightly toasted on one side.

2. ....
   Now thinly butter the untoasted side of each and then spread a thicker layer of tomato paste on the top.

3. ....
   Now add whatever toppings you prefer and finish off with a small amount of grated cheese in the middle of each.

4. ....
   Finally, place your mini-pizzas under the grill until the cheese has melted nicely.

HELLO KITTY'S
TOP TIP
....
Keep your ingredients in the centre of your pizzas as far as possible so that you can still see the decorative shape around the edge.

97

Cheeky Cheese Straws

Cheese straws are really simple to make and they are perfect with dips like hummus and salsa.

Ingredients:

- 320g ready-rolled puff pastry
- 250g of cheddar cheese
- A little plain flour

You will need:

- Cheese grater
- Rolling pin
- Knife
- Baking tray

1. ....
   Pre-heat your oven to 220°C/ Gas Mark 8.

2. ....
   Lay out your sheet of pastry on a clean surface, dusted with flour.

3. ....
   Grate enough cheddar cheese to sprinkle over the top of one half (about three handfuls is perfect).

4. ....
   When the cheese is on top of the pastry, fold over the empty half, then roll it out again, making sure you have spinkled more flour on your surface first.

5. ....
   Now cut your pastry into strips, about 2cm thick, then twist them around to make a tight spiral.

6. ....
   Place your strips on a non-stick baking tray about 2cm apart and scatter over any left-over cheese. Bake on the middle shelf for 14 minutes, or until they are golden on top!

HELLO KITTY'S
TOP TIP
. . . .
Cheese straws always get eaten quickly so make sure you have enough for everybody!

Mmm–ushroom Cups

These make a delicious savoury bite-sized snack.
They're great for vegetarian guests, too.

Ingredients:
- Mushrooms
- Goat's cheese
- Olive oil

You will need:
- Spoon
- Baking tray

1. ....
Give your mushrooms a good clean in cold water and dry them.

2. ....
Carefully pull the stems off your mushrooms, so you are left with just the cup. Now drizzle with olive oil.

3. ....
Spoon some goat's cheese (or any soft white cheese if you don't like goat's) into the cup.

4. ....
Place on a baking tray and pop them under the grill until the cheese starts to bubble.

5. ....
Serve them warm!

Sublime Sandwiches

Choose your fillings from the list below. Make your sandwiches, then cut them into small rectangles. Cut off the crusts to make them look extra-elegant!

CUCUMBER & cream cheese

Peel your cucumber and slice thinly. Spread a layer of cream cheese and arrange your cucumber on top. Fresh and delicious!

JAM AND PEANUT BUTTER

This sweet treat is a must for those who can't wait for cakes! Use a thin layer of each spread so you don't overload the bread.

EGG AND CRESS

This is a classic combination and super-yummy. Boil some eggs for around seven minutes (you may need longer for larger eggs). Leave them to cool, then carefully peel off the shells. Mash the boiled eggs and add a teaspoon of mayonnaise or salad cream to bind it all together. Mix in a handful of fresh cress.

SMOKED SALMON

This super-sophisticated choice is the easiest to make, too! Simply place a layer of the salmon on buttered, brown bread and slice. Smoked salmon can be quite expensive, so you don't have to make too many of these!

TUNA AND SWEETCORN

Empty and drain a tin of tuna into a bowl and break up with a fork. Add a heaped tablespoonful of mayonnaise and two to three teaspoons of sweetcorn and give it a good mix.

CHICKEN SALAD

Place pieces of sliced, cooked chicken onto your bread, followed by some fresh lettuce and tomato for a simple, fresh sandwich.

SANDWICH LOLLIPOPS!

Roll out a cream cheese sandwich with a rolling pin until it's thin and flat, then roll it up into a sausage shape, wrap tightly with clingfilm and pop in the fridge. After about half an hour, take it out and cut discs off it. You can add wooden kebab sticks to make it look like a lolly!

Dinky Jacket Potatoes

These mini jacket potatoes look really cute on the plate. Once you've mastered the technique, why not try different toppings?

Ingredients:
- New potatoes
- Cottage or cream cheese
- Chives
- Olive oil
- Pinch of salt

You will need:
- Baking tray
- Small bowl
- Spoon
- Pastry brush

1. Pre-heat your oven to 190°C/ Gas Mark 5. Take your potatoes and give them a wash if needed. Pat dry and brush with a little olive oil and a light sprinkling of salt.

2. Place them on a baking tray and cook for 25 minutes, or until they have gone lovely and golden.

3. ....
While they are cooking, carefully chop your chives into small pieces and mix with the cheese to make your filling.

4. ....
Once your potatoes have cooked and cooled slightly, carefully cut a small slit in the top of each one and fill with your cheese -and-chive mixture.

Scrummy Scotch Eggs

Super-swish department store, Fortnum and Mason, invented these scrumptious snacks over 300 years ago!

Ingredients:
- 400g sausage meat
- 6 medium-sized hard-boiled eggs
- 100g breadcrumbs
- 1 egg, beaten
- Salt and pepper to taste

You will need:
- 2 bowls
- Baking tray

1. ....
   Pre-heat your oven to 190°C/ Gas Mark 5.

2. ....
   Split your sausage meat into 6 equal balls, then pat flat on a clean, lightly floured surface.

3. ....
   Making sure there is no shell left on your eggs, wrap each piece of sausage meat around each one. This can be a bit tricky, but try and make sure there are no gaps.

4. ....

Place your beaten egg into a bowl, and roll each scotch egg in it, then place the breadcrumbs in another bowl, and roll each egg in them until it is covered.

5. ....

Pop your scotch eggs on a baking tray, season, and place them in the oven for 35-40 minutes, or until they are brown.

HELLO KITTY'S
TOP TIP
....

Turn your eggs over half-way through cooking, so that they become brown all over!

The Ultimate Cupcakes!

The best thing about cupcakes is that you can really be creative! Start with these vanilla cakes, then turn the page for more delicious flavours.

Ingredients:

Makes about 9

For the cakes

- 110g butter or margarine, softened at room temperature
- 110g caster sugar
- 2 eggs
- 1 tsp vanilla extract
- 110g self-raising flour
- 1-2 tbsp milk

For the buttercream icing

- 140g soft butter
- 280g icing sugar
- 1-2 tbsp milk

You will need:

- Cupcake cases
- Cupcake tray
- Bowl
- Mixing spoon
- Tablespoon and teaspoon
- Weighing scales
- Whisk or fork

1. ....
   Pre-heat your oven to 180°C/
   Gas Mark 4, then pop your
   cupcake cases into the wells in
   the cupcake tray.

2. ....
   Cream the butter and sugar
   together – this just means
   mixing and beating really well
   until the mixture is pale and
   fluffy (you can use a electric
   whisk if you have one).

3. ....
   Whisk your eggs and vanilla
   extract together, then add them to
   the creamed butter and sugar.*
   Once these ingredients are
   combined, slowly stir the flour
   in. Next stir the milk in bit by bit.

4. ....
   When all the ingredients are
   completely combined, add
   a heaped tablespoon of the
   mixture to each cupcake case.

*If you are making flavoured cupcakes,
turn the page now for special instructions.

5. ....
   Bake in the oven for 20-25
   minutes, or until the cakes are
   lightly golden on top. Cool on a
   wire baking tray.

6. ....
   To make the buttercream icing,
   beat the butter, half the icing
   sugar and milk until smooth,
   then add the other half of the
   sugar and mix again. If you are
   making flavoured icing, check
   the recipes overleaf before
   you begin.

Cute Cupcake Flavours

*Once you've mastered the basic cupcake,
it's time to get creative with the flavours!*

STRAWBERRY

For strawberry-flavoured cakes, add small chunks of strawberry to your cake mix and use the strawberry juice instead of milk in your icing. You could also add a few drops of red food colouring to make your icing turn pink!

CHOCOLATE

Before you mix in your flour, take out one heaped tablespoon and replace with cocoa. For chocolate buttercream icing, add 75g of melted chocolate to your finished buttercream and stir well. Use a fine grater to grate some chocolate on top of your icing, too.

LEMON

Add the zest of one lemon to your cupcake recipe, plus a squeeze of juice to your buttercream, instead of milk. You can even sprinkle some zest on top of your cakes for extra zing!

APPLE AND CINNAMON

To combine these gorgeous flavours, make cinnamon cupcakes and apple-flavoured icing. Simply add 2 teaspoons of cinnamon to your flour before mixing with the wet ingredients. For apple buttercream icing, use apple sauce from a jar instead of milk (you may need to add more icing sugar to make the cream stiff).

COCONUT AND BANANA

Give your cupcakes a banana flavour by adding one mashed-up banana to your cake mix before baking. Add a couple of drops of coconut extract to your icing as you beat the butter and icing sugar together. Taste your icing as you go to make sure the flavour isn't too strong. If you can't find coconut extract, halve the icing quantities and stir in 1 tbsp of coconut cream.

Scrumptious Scones

These little cakes can be sweet or savoury
– just make a small change to the recipe!

Ingredients:

Makes 6-8

- 225g self-raising flour
- 50g butter, straight from the fridge
- 1 tsp baking powder
- A pinch of salt
- 120ml milk
- 25g caster sugar (remove for savoury scones)
- 50g sultanas (or 50g cheddar cheese for savoury scones) – both of these are optional

You will need:

- Mixing bowl
- Rolling pin
- Round cookie cutter

1. ....
   Pre-heat your oven to 200°C/ Gas Mark 6.

2. ....
   Put the flour and salt in a bowl, then carefully chop the butter into cubes and add to the bowl. Rub the mixture together with your fingers until it looks

like breadcrumbs. Then add the sugar and sultanas if you are making sweet scones, or the cheese if you are making savoury ones.

3. ....
Add the milk and stir until your mixture comes together in a ball.

4. ....
Roll the ball out on a floured surface until it is about 2cm thick. Use your cookie cutter to cut the scone shapes and place them on a lightly greased baking tray.

5. ....
Bake for 15 minutes, or until they have risen and the top has gone golden brown.

Chocolate Strawberries

A super-simple, but really delicious addition to your table!

Ingredients:

- 12 strawberries – washed and dried
- 100g chocolate (white, milk or dark)

You will need:

- Kebab sticks or skewers
- Heatproof bowl
- Saucepan
- Tray with baking paper

1. ....
   Melt the chocolate in a heatproof bowl placed over a pan of simmering water or melt in the microwave.

2. ....
   Place your strawberries on the skewer one at a time and dip halfway into the chocolate.

3. ....
   Carefully slide your strawberries off the skewer on to the baking paper to cool and put in the fridge until hard.

4. ....
   Arrange on a pretty plate!

HELLO KITTY'S
TOP TIP
. . . .

This treat is so easy to do, and
looks super-cute placed on a
saucer, next to a fruity drink!

Hello Kitty's Perfect Brownies

Everyone loves these bite-sized chocolate treats and they are super-easy to make!

Ingredients:

- 170g dark chocolate
- 115g unsalted butter softened to room temperature
- 225g soft brown sugar
- 1 tsp vanilla extract
- 2 eggs
- 170g plain flour
- 100g chocolate chips

You will need:

- 2 mixing bowls
- Spoon
- Baking tray
- Saucepan
- Heatproof bowl

1. ....

   Pre-heat your oven to 180°C/ Gas Mark 4.

2. ....

   Carefully melt the chocolate in a heatproof bowl over a pan of simmering water. Alternatively, you can melt the chocolate in a microwave.

3. ....
   Mix the butter and sugar together in a separate bowl, then stir in the melted chocolate.

4. ....
   Beat the eggs and vanilla extract together in a different bowl, then add to your mixture. Add the flour and chocolate chips and stir well.

5. ....
   Pour your mixture into a baking tin. Make sure the mixture is even across the tin.

6. ....
   Place your tin in the oven for 20-25 minutes.

7. ....
   When they have cooled, cut the brownies into small squares. Mmm!

Choccy Cornflake Nests

Once you've made your nests you can fill them with anything from fruit to marshmallows!

Ingredients:
- 100g chocolate
- 50g butter
- 3 tbsp golden syrup
- 75g cornflakes
- Marshmallows, chocolate eggs... or anything you like!

You will need:
- Large mixing bowl and spoon
- Heatproof bowl
- About 15 cupcake cases

1. ....
Melt the chocolate, butter and golden syrup together in a heat-proof bowl over a pan of simmering water, or melt in a microwave.

2. ....
Take the chocolate sauce off the heat and mix in your cornflakes until they are all covered.

3. ....
Spoon some of the mixture into each cupcake case and make a hollow in the middle, like a nest.

4. ....
Once cooled you can fill your nests with anything you like!

HELLO KITTY'S
TOP TIP

These little treats would
be great at an Easter-
themed tea party.

RECIPES

Whoopie Pies

*These scrummy biscuits are delicious
– "whoopie" for whoopie pies!*

Ingredients:

- 270g plain flour
- 40g cocoa powder
- 1 tsp baking powder
- 190g caster sugar
- 120g butter, softened
- 2 eggs
- 1 tsp vanilla extract
- 250ml full fat milk
- The buttercream recipe from p.108!

You will need:

- Mixing bowl and spoon
- Whisk or fork
- Baking tray
- Teaspoon and tablespoon

1. ....
   Pre-heat your oven to 180°C. Mix or 'cream' the butter and sugar together until they are pale and smooth. Whisk together the eggs and gradually mix into the creamed butter.

2.   ....
Mix the flour, cocoa and baking powder together in a bowl, then gradually add to the creamed butter. Add a little of the dry ingredients, then a little milk and repeat until everything is mixed together well.

3.   ....
Place 50 pence-sized dollops of the mixture to your baking tray, making sure there are an even number as these will make the two halves of your 'pie'.

4.   ....
Pop them in the oven for 15 minutes, or until they are springy to touch. Meanwhile, make the buttercream icing.

5.   ....
When your pie halves are cooked, leave them to cool on a wire rack. Once cooled, spread some cream onto the flat side of one half, then pop another half on top! Yum.

HELLO KITTY'S
TOP TIP
....
Dust with icing sugar for a professional finishing touch.

121

Cute Coconut Cubes

These pretty pink squares would make a great party favour!

Ingredients:
- 250g sweetened condensed milk
- 250g icing sugar
- 200g desiccated coconut
- Red or pink food colouring

You will need:
- 2 mixing bowls and spoon
- Clingfilm
- Square plastic container

1. ....
Mix together the condensed milk and icing sugar. It takes a while, but keep going until the mixture becomes really thick.

2. ....
Add the coconut and keep mixing until it is all combined, then split the mixture in two.

3. ....
Add a couple of drops of food colouring to one batch to make it pink.

4. ....
Now line your container with clingfilm, making sure there's about 5cm hanging over the sides.

HELLO KITTY'S
TOP TIP
....

Arrange these in a
chequerboard design for an
Alice in Wonderland party!

5. ....

Place the first batch in the container and squish it down so it's flat. Now layer the second batch on top in the same way.

6. ....

Put in the fridge for 3 hours to set, then cut into squares – cute!

Butterfly Cakes

Turn a plain sponge into
a beautiful butterfly!

Ingredients:

Makes 12

- The cupcake and buttercream recipes from p.108
- Icing sugar to decorate
- Edible glitter (optional)

You will need:

- Knife
- A pretty serving plate or cake stand

1. ....
   Make the cupcakes, using the recipe on p.108

2. ....
   Once they have cooled, carefully slice the raised top of each cake so that you have a flat surface. Make sure you keep the top in one piece!

3. ....
   Now make the buttercream icing from p.109 or check out the flavours on p.110.

4. ....
   Place a dollop of the buttercream icing onto the flat surface. Now cut the top of your cake in half and squidge them into the buttercream at 45° angles – so they look like wings!

5. ....
   Sprinkle with icing sugar and edible glitter (if you're using it) and arrange on a pretty cake stand, then eat them before they flutter away!

HELLO KITTY'S
TOP TIP
....
Chocolate and vanilla ones look great arranged on a plate next to each other.

Lavender Shortbread

Using lavender sugar gives these little biscuits a delicious floral flavour.

Ingredients:
- 125g lavender caster sugar
- 225g unsalted butter
- 300g plain flour
- 50g ground rice

You will need:
- Baking tray
- Sieve
- Spoon
- Bowls
- Cookie cutters (a 6cm diameter cookie cutter makes about 30 biscuits)

1. ....
Pre-heat your oven to 180°C/ Gas Mark 4.

2. ....
Sieve your sugar into a bowl to catch all the lavender seeds. Pop them out of the way as you'll need them later!

3. ....
Cream the butter and sugar together until it looks smooth and fluffy. Add the flour, ground rice and lavender seeds and mix together.

4. ....
When your mixture starts to look a bit like breadcrumbs, it's time to use your hands! Dust them in a little flour, then start working your mixture into a dough.

5. ....
Here's the important bit! Once your mixture has turned into a dough, you need to leave it to cool for 15 minutes in the fridge!

6. ....
Now, roll out your dough to about 1cm thickness and cut out your biscuit shapes. Place them on a baking tray and pop them back in the fridge for another 15 minutes.

7. ....
Bake your shortbread for 15-20 minutes, or until they start to turn golden. Yummy!

HELLO KITTY'S
TOP TIP
....
Most supermarkets sell lavender sugar, but if you have a lavender plant in bloom, use a tbsp of seeds from that and ordinary caster sugar.

Jam Polka Dots

Arrange these treats on a large plate to get a really cute polka dot effect!

Ingredients:

Makes 20

- 225g salted butter, softened
- 100g caster sugar
- 250g plain flour
- Jam of your choice

You will need:

- Mixing bowl
- Spoon
- Baking tray

1. Pre-heat your oven to 190°C/ Gas Mark 5. Mix the butter, sugar and flour together in a bowl until it forms a dough, then roll into balls just smaller than a ping pong ball.

2. Place the balls on a baking tray about 3cm apart and push down with your thumb to make a well in the middle of each one.

3. Spoon your favourite jam into the well!

4. Bake in the oven for 15-20 mins, leave to cool, then dust with icing sugar.

Rocky Road Squares

These squares are perfect if you're using the oven for something else, as they don't need any baking at all!

Ingredients:

- 200g dark or milk chocolate
- 100g of butter (unsalted is best)
- 100g of mini marshmallows
- 75g of raisins
- 100g of digestive biscuits (broken into little chunks)

You will need:

- A baking tin (18cm square is perfect, if you have it)
- Heatproof bowl
- Spoon
- Saucepan

1. ••••••••••••••••••••••••••••••
   Carefully melt the chocolate and butter together in a heatproof bowl over a pan of simmering water. This stops the chocolate burning as it melts. Alternatively, you can melt the chocolate in a microwave.

2. ••••••••••••••••••••••••••••••
   Take your chocolate and butter off the heat and add in your marshmallows, raisins and digestive biscuits.

3. ••••••••••••••••••••••••••••••
   Rub some butter around your baking tin, or line with baking paper if you have it. Pour the mixture into your tin.

4. ••••••••••••••••••••••••••••••
   Pop the tin into the fridge to set for about 2 to 3 hours. Once set, cut into squares.

HELLO KITTY'S
TOP TIP
••••••••••••••••••••
Only take your Rocky Road out of the fridge just before you are ready to serve – otherwise it might melt!

Hello Kitty's Banana Bread

Once baked, this bread is great
toasted with butter on top. Yum!

Ingredients:

- 125g butter
- 150g caster sugar
- 1 tsp vanilla extract
- 1 egg, beaten
- 2 ripe bananas, mashed
- 190g self-raising flour
- 60ml milk

What you need:

- Mixing bowl
- Spoon
- Fork
- Loaf tin

1. ....
   Pre-heat your oven to 150°C/ Gas Mark 2

2. ....
   Carefully melt the butter in a pan.

3. ....
   Mix the butter, sugar and vanilla together in a bowl until it's light and smooth.

4. ....
   Mash your bananas with the back of a fork. (It's fine to leave a few lumps in).

5. ....
Mix the bananas, egg, flour and milk with the butter and sugar until it is all combined and looking smooth.

6. ....
Pour the mixture into your loaf tin, then carefully place it in the oven for 45-55 minutes or until it's golden brown.

Delicious Drinks

Don't overlook the drinks when planning the refreshments for your party! Nothing beats a glass of lovely cold water when you're really thirsty, but these liquid treats taste gorgeous and you can make them look extra-special with these sweet twists!

STRAW NAME TAGS

Personalise each drink with these cute straw decorations. Photocopy or trace this template onto paper – make sure you do enough for each of your guests. Write their name in the space, then wrap around your straw. Secure with paper glue. Adorable!

Write their name here!

WHO NEEDS GLASSES?

For a really cool look ditch plain old glasses and use something else instead! Little vases, glass bottles and tea-cups all look really sweet.

SCRUMPTIOUS MASTS

You can get brightly coloured cocktail stirrers, or even just plain wooden skewer kebabs from most supermarkets – pop yummy-looking sweets, berries or grapes on the end to give your drink extra wow.

BOW-TASTIC

Wrap a length of lace or ribbon around each glass and tie with a bow for a super-cute feel.

HELLO KITTY'S TOP TIP

Why not use adorable little paper cocktail parasols, available from most supermarkets, to decorate your delicious concoction?

Tremendous Tea

There's nothing like a cup of tea to go with your cake – that warm melt-in-the-mouth moment. And not only does everyone take theirs differently (milk in first or after?) there are so many different kinds of tea to try! Take a look at the chart opposite and select the best type for your party.

Always ask an adult to help you around boiling water!

Name	What's it like?
Breakfast tea	This is the classic tea that most people will have tasted. It's lovely with a drop of milk (and sugar if you like!).
Earl Grey	This is flavoured with bergamot, which is a bit like orange, so it has a slightly fruity taste.
Darjeeling	Darjeeling is named after the town in India where the tea leaves are grown. It has a delicate taste and golden colour.
Assam	This strong tea has a faint flavour of chocolate.
Chai	This was the favourite tea of the Indian royal family. It's spicy and warming.
Herbal tea	There are lots of herbal teas to choose from, so you may need to try a few to get the one you like. They don't contain caffeine which means you can drink as much as you like!
Green tea	Green tea has a fresh taste and contains antioxidants which are really good for you!

Home-made Hot Choc

Perfect for winter tea parties or friends who don't really like tea!

Ingredients:
- 450g of sugar
- 250g cocoa
- 1 tbsp salt
- 15 fl oz milk

You will need:
- Empty jar
- Mixing bowl
- Whisk
- Saucepan

1. ....
Mix all the ingredients together in a bowl.

2. ....
Place your ingredients in a jar with a sealable lid.

3. ....
Warm the milk, then add a little to two tablespoons of the chocolate powder and mix into a paste. Stir in the remaining milk, then whisk it round until it's bubbly and frothy, before pouring into your mug.

HELLO KITTY'S
TOP TIP
Add whipped cream,
marshmallows and a sprinkle
of extra cocoa powder on top to
finish off your perfect drink!

Chocolate Stirrers

*A pretty way to make any drink
instantly scrumptious!*

You will need:

- Chocolate to melt
- Ice-cube trays
- Lollipop sticks (if you can't
  find these, you can use halved
  wooden kebab skewers or coffee
  stirrers)

HELLO KITTY'S
TOP TIP

Give each of your guests a mug full
of warm milk and a stirrer, then
watch as you all make delicious
chocolate milk!

1. ••••••••••••••••••••••••••••••••
   Melt your chocolate in a heatproof bowl over a pan of simmering water or melt it in a microwave.

2. ••••••••••••••••••••••••••••••••
   Spoon the chocolate into your ice-cube tray. Fill almost to the top and wipe away any spills.

3. ••••••••••••••••••••••••••••••••
   Leave to set somewhere cool, but don't put them in the fridge as they might go too hard!

4. ••••••••••••••••••••••••••••••••
   When they are not quite set, push a lollipop stick in the middle of each ice-cube tray – these will make the handles for your stirrers.

HELLO KITTY'S
TOP TIP
••••••••••••••••••••••••••
These also make great lollipops to give guests as they leave, or to have on the side as an extra nibble.

Hello Kitty's Fizzy Floats

Hello Kitty loves making these ice cream treats on hot summer days. Your guests will love them, too!

You will need:
- Tall glasses
- Straws
- Lemonade or cola
- Ice cream

1. ....
Ice cream floats are super easy to make, and taste delicious, too! All you have to do is choose your flavour combination, then pour your chosen drink in a tall glass until it is about ⅔ full.

2. ....
Next, place a scoop of ice cream on top and push a straw through the middle until it reaches the drink.

FLAVOURS!
....
- Lemonade + strawberry
- Lemonade + vanilla
- Cola + chocolate
- Cola + cherry

HELLO KITTY'S
TOP TIP
Keep spoons handy so your
guests can scoop up the rest of
the ice cream from their glasses.

RECIPES

Sparkling Fruit Punch

If you don't fancy tea, there are plenty of other drinks you can try, and this one is extra-special!

You will need:

- Cranberry juice
- Apple juice (not cloudy)
- Cranberries
- Sliced fruit
- Edible gold glitter
- A large bowl or jug

1. ....
In a large bowl or jug, mix together two parts cranberry juice to one part apple juice. For example, if you put in two glasses of cranberry juice, only put in one glass of apple – you want it to look red!

2. ....
Next add your edible gold glitter. This will turn your drink into a gorgeous, glittering cocktail! Add just enough to make your punch shimmer.

3. ....
When you serve your drinks, add a few cranberries to the glass. They will soak up the juice and make a yummy treat when the drink is finished.

HELLO KITTY'S
TOP TIP

The glitter will slowly settle at the bottom of your jug or bowl, so make sure you give it a stir before serving to make sure each drink glitters!

Fruity Cubes

These cute little cubes will make drinks cool,
add a fruity twist and look really cute!

You will need:
- Ice cube tray
- Blueberries, grapes or strawberries
- Water

1. ....
   Ask a grown up to help you chop your fruit into small pieces. The fruit should be small enough to fit in your tray with room around the edges. You shouldn't need to chop the blueberries!

2. ....
   Pop a piece of fruit into each section of an ice-cube tray, then top up with water.

3. ....
   Place your tray in the freezer to set, then turn them out and add to any cold drink at your party. Cute!

HELLO KITTY'S
TOP TIP

These are best in clear drinks
like lemonade or water so you
can really see them!

SAYING GOODBYE

Party's over – time to say goodbye! When you're waving your guests off, you could do it in style with little party bags (check out the homemade ones on p.58) filled with sweets, any left-over cakes and biscuits. You could even pop in a personal message to each friend thanking them for coming.

Then flop in a chair and have a cup of tea and one last biscuit before you begin the dreaded tidying up!

Time to say goodbye to you too! Hello Kitty really hopes you've enjoyed and been inspired by all her party wisdom. Here's wishing you the best party ever, whatever you choose to do – and if you only take one piece of advice from this book then let it be this: HAVE FUN! After all, that's what parties are all about!

Ciao!

Hello Kitty

x

NOTES

Use these pages for notes on the following sections, to make sure you have everything ready for your big day!

- Guests
- Invitations
- Decorations
- Equipment
- Party plan
- Shopping list

- Outfit
- Music
- Table settings
- Party bags
- Favours
- Anything else!

NOTES

....

NOTES

NOTES

NOTES

NOTES

NOTES
....

NOTES

. . . .

NOTES